AMERICAN OUTLAWS

Adam Seidel

BROADWAY PLAY PUBLISHING INC
New York
www.broadwayplaypublishing.com
info@broadwayplaypublishing.com

AMERICAN OUTLAWS
© Copyright 2023 Adam Seidel

Cover photo by Adam Seidel

First edition: January 2023
I S B N: 978-0-88145-961-6

Book design: Marie Donovan
Page make-up: Adobe InDesign
Typeface: Palatino

AMERICAN OUTLAWS received its world premiere at Saint Louis Actors' Studio in July, 2016. The cast and creative contributors were:

MIKE ....David Wassilak
MITCH..Eric Dean White

Director...John Piersen

AMERICAN OUTLAWS was subsequently produced in New York City at 59E59 by Saint Louis Actors' Studio in January, 2017. The cast and creative contributors were:

MIKE ....Justin Ivan Brown
MITCH..Eric Dean White

Director...John Piersen

CHARACTERS

MIKE
"RON"/MITCH COHEN
SUSAN COHEN

Scene 1

(The inside of a small cafe. At a table sits MIKE, *an early forties unassuming guy, reading a book. After a moment, "*RON*", a man of slightly older age, enters. He pretends to be calm but he's unsure of himself. He's carrying a paper bag. "*RON*" watches* MIKE, *who faces away from him, inquisitive if* MIKE *knows he's there.* MIKE *knows he's there. After a moment "*RON*" takes a seat at a table behind* MIKE. *They sit back to back.)*

MIKE: Don't waste another person's time. That's something my father used to say. He was a very stringent man. Always on time. It was his upbringing. A slave to the clock.

RON: I don't understand.

MIKE: It's twelve thirty two. You're two minutes late.

(Pause)

RON: You must be Michael.

MIKE: And you're Ron.

RON: Yes. *(Beat)* I'm, Ron.

MIKE: I'm guessing Ron's not your real name.

RON: How could you tell?

MIKE: You don't strike me as a Ron. Plus the way you said it sounds like you think you're in a spy movie.

RON: Michael's not your real name either, is it?

MIKE: How did you know?

RON: "Michael" strikes me as a bit formal. The only people who refer to themselves formally are sports stars or celebrities.

MIKE: This is true.

RON: Also, The archangel is named Michael. He descends from heaven and gives each soul the chance to redeem itself before passing. *(Beat)* I thought maybe that's why you called yourself Michael. Like an superhero identity.

MIKE: You've given this some thought, haven't you?

RON: I like to analyze things.

MIKE: "Michael" was the first name that came to my head.

RON: That's not very exciting.

MIKE: Come sit with me.

RON: Should I?

MIKE: It might make things easier.

("RON" gets up and sits in MIKE's table.)

RON: What are you reading?

MIKE: *Don Quixote.* Ever read it?

RON: I saw the movie with John Lithgow.

MIKE: Good actor.

RON: Who's your favorite character?

MIKE: Who's yours?

RON: I like Sancho Panza. *(Beat)* He knows he's superior to Don Quixote but also realizes that without him Quixote would be completely lost. So he plays along and remains the humble servant. Kinda admirable. Don't you think?

MIKE: How is that admirable?

RON: He possesses knowledge that would crush Quixote but he doesn't act on it.

MIKE: Which makes him a coward. *(He puts down the book and looks at "*RON*".)*

RON: So how do we do this?

MIKE: You give me a bag containing ten thousand dollars and a picture of the target, and soon after they have a horrible accident resulting in their death.

RON: You mean you, kill them.

MIKE: Ron, do you know what a moron is?

RON: A person who lacks intelligence.

MIKE: The dictionary defines "moron" as a grown adult who possesses the intelligence of an eight to ten year old. *(Beat)* Do I strike you as a moron?

RON: Of course not. I don't even know you.

MIKE: There's this memory from my childhood that's always stuck with me. I was ten. There was this boy in my class, Jimmy. Jimmy came from a decent family and always had very fancy birthday parties. Every year he'd invite everyone in my class except me. Being that I was ten I became sensitive to the fact that I was being excluded, so my mother called up his mother. The next day at school Jimmy handed me an invitation. The ice cream parlour, Saturday at noon. Saturday, I go to the ice cream parlour and no one is there. I go to the counter and ask the owner Mister Kimball when Jimmy's birthday party begins. Do you know what he tells me? That the party happened the night before. I felt very foolish at the time, but now I look on it as a valuable lesson. See, it wasn't little Jimmy that made me look like a fool. It was me. I had let my emotions put me in a position of vulnerability. After that day I vowed it would never happen again.

RON: What happened to little Jimmy?

MIKE: He died.

RON: Did you kill him?

MIKE: Why would I kill him? I was a child.

RON: I'm sorry.

MIKE: Relax. It was a valid question. *(Beat)* One could call Jimmy's death an inevitable act of fate. By the end of high school little Jimmy's future was pretty much sealed, working dead end jobs. He eventually got hired as a technician with the telephone company. One winter night he was up a poll, drunk. Jimmy slipped and broke his neck. They didn't find Jimmy for a few weeks. When they did, the animals had gotten to him. Matter of fact the only things left on his body were a torn pair of jeans and a work glove. May I see your gun?

RON: What makes you think I have a gun?

MIKE: Don't insult my intelligence.

RON: I don't have a gun.

MIKE: You've got a revolver tucked into your right pocket. I'm not going to ask you again.

RON: What if someone sees it?

MIKE: We're the only people here.

RON: Where are servers? The cooks?

MIKE: All on break. The owner is an old friend of mine. From time to time he lets me use the place.

(After a moment "RON" takes a small revolver and puts it on the table. MIKE inspects it.)

RON: I'm sorry I lied.

MIKE: I don't like apologies. Now why'd you bring the gun?

RON: I thought that I should have one.

MIKE: Why would you, in this situation, feel the need to have a gun?

RON: Given the nature of this meeting, I felt I should have protection.

MIKE: From me?

RON: I mean especially considering who you are and what you do, not that I have a problem with your line of work. I just felt more comfortable knowing that I had it.

MIKE: For protection.

RON: Yes.

MIKE: Or an execution. *(Indicating himself)*

RON: I think there's been a misunderstanding. *(He stands up.)*

MIKE: We're not finished talking.

RON: Let's just pretend this never happened.

(MIKE levels the gun at "RON".)

MIKE: Ron if you don't sit down I'm going to blow your head off.

("RON" sits down.)

MIKE: Where did you buy this gun?

RON: I'd rather not say.

MIKE: Whoever sold it to you is a complete amateur. The grip is exposed so prints can be lifted. Not to mention the serial number isn't even scratched off.

RON: I don't see why that matters.

MIKE: Use your head, Ron. If this gun has been used in other murders, and I'm going to take a stab and say it has, then all those incidents could be put on you.

RON: I thought that was just in movies.

MIKE: Fiction comes from truth. You know who said that?

RON: I don't know.

MIKE: Take a guess.

RON: Dean Martin.

MIKE: Is that a serious answer?

RON: Your father.

MIKE: My father?

RON: Father's say stuff like that.

MIKE: Stuff like what?

RON: They say things that are poignant.

MIKE: Do you know what poignant means?

RON: It means touching. Affecting.

MIKE: And what about the phrase "Fiction comes from truth" is touching or affecting?

RON: Nothing.

MIKE: Then why did you say it?

RON: I don't know! I'm sorry.

MIKE: I told you not to apologize.

RON: Sorry…I'm nervous and poignant was the first word that came to mind.

MIKE: There's no reason to be nervous. We're just two guys sitting in an empty restaurant with a gun. Now take another guess.

RON: I have no idea who said it!

MIKE: My uncle Johnny. He told me that right before he died. Would you like to know how my Uncle Johnny died? *(Beat)* He was sitting in his living room, watching his favorite show on TV, *Wheel of Fortune*, eating his favorite meal, Salisbury steak and red roasted potatoes.

RON: Your uncle's favorite meal was Salisbury steak?

MIKE: He was a man of simple pleasures.

RON: How'd he die?

MIKE: A seven millimeter bullet came whizzing through his window and went right through his head.

RON: How do you know that?

MIKE: Because I shot it from a car across the street.

RON: You killed your uncle?

MIKE: You're not judging me, are you Ron?

RON: Why would you kill your uncle?

MIKE: There's an order to things. And those of us who don't adhere to the order must be punished. Do you know why?

RON: No.

MIKE: Because we must to protect the order. If we don't protect it, then it will fall apart. And what do we have if we don't have order? *(He reaches into the bag and pulls out a wad of money and a picture.)* You actually brought money and a picture.

RON: I figured you'd of found it suspicious if I hadn't.

MIKE: Very admirable. This is an old picture of Susan.

RON: It's the one I keep in my wallet.

MIKE: Where'd you take it?

RON: On our honeymoon.

MIKE: Where did you go?

RON: Pie de la Cuesta. *(Beat)* It's a little coastal town in Mexico.

MIKE: Excellent seafood in Pie de la Cuesta. There's a little restaurant right on the beach where the owner is also the chef. I call it a restaurant but really it's a slab of concrete with a tarp over it. You sit down he brings you a beer and tells you "Espera." You know that espera means?

RON: Wait.

MIKE: Exactly. The boats haven't come in yet so there is no fish to eat. So you and him both sit there, you sipping your cervaza and him playing his guitar, singing love songs about his deceased wife. I don't know if it's the atmosphere or the sound of his voice underscored by the crashing waves but the experience is enchanting. And just when you thought it couldn't get any better the boats arrive. They drive right up on the beach no more than thirty feet from where you're sitting, then the fishermen hop out and deliver their catch. Then for the equivalent of five dollars, you eat the most delicious food this great Earth has to offer. It's an experience one never forgets.

(MIKE *picks up* "RON"'s *revolver. He opens the cylinder and lets the bullets fall onto the table. He takes one bullet, puts it into the gun and closes the cylinder.*)

MIKE: I'm going to ask you a series of questions. And every time you lie to me I'm going to pull the trigger which may or may not kill you. (*Beat*) What is your name?

RON: Ron.

(MIKE *pulls the trigger. It goes click.*)

MIKE: I don't know what part of "if you lie to me I'll shoot you," you didn't understand, but I assure you I was quite serious.

MITCH: Mitch.

MIKE: Mitch what?

MITCH: Cohen.

MIKE: What's your address, Mitch Cohen?

MITCH: 2346 Newhall Lane. Trenton.

MIKE: What is your vocation?

MITCH: I'm a CPA.

MIKE: Where is your office?

MITCH: 45 West 22nd street.

MIKE: What floor?

MITCH: Fifth.

MIKE: It's a good floor to be on. Not too low, not high enough that you can't escape a fire. *(Beat)* I like your art work by the way.

MITCH: What art work?

MIKE: The Keith Haring behind your desk.

MITCH: You've been in my office?

MIKE: The painting is called "Hear No Evil, See No Evil." It's a brilliant example of balanced composition. Did you know he lived in a box in central park for two years?

MITCH: Who?

MIKE: Keith Haring. That's who we've been discussing.

MITCH: You're thinking of Jean Michelle Basquiat. He was another New York painter from the eighties.

(MIKE *pulls the trigger. It goes click.)*

MITCH: What was that for?!

MIKE: I don't like being corrected. *(Beat)* What kind of car do you drive?

MITCH: Why does that matter?

MIKE: We're running out of chambers, Mitch. *(He readies the gun.)*

MITCH: A LEXUS! I drive a Lexus!

MIKE: Does it get good gas milage?

MITCH: It's not terrible.

(Beat)

MIKE: That concludes the warm up round. You didn't do poorly, but from here on out I suggest you answer every question correctly. Are you ready? *(Beat)* Nod or shake your head.

(MITCH nods.)

MIKE: Aside from your duties as a CPA, you work for a certain organization.

MITCH: I do work for a lot of organizations.

MIKE: But this organization is more of a family. Whose last name ends in a vowel.

MITCH: ...I don't think I should answer that.

MIKE: You work for Dominic Callabro. *(Beat)* I want to hear you say it.

MITCH: Why?

MIKE: Because I want us to be thorough. And to do that we need to cover all the bases.

MITCH: He's a friend.

MIKE: Dominic Collabro is your friend.

MITCH: And sometimes I help him with certain things. As a friend.

MIKE: You launder his money.

MITCH: I occasionally move funds from one place to the other.

MIKE: That's called laundering.

MITCH: Okay. Fine. I launder his money.

MIKE: For how long have you done this?

MITCH: Three years.

MIKE: How did you and Dominic meet? School buddies? Play on the same softball team? Perhaps you're both in the choir at church.

MITCH: We met at a card game.

MIKE: When you asked Dominic to contact me on your behalf, what did you tell him?

MITCH: I said I needed your services.

MIKE: You asked for me specifically?

MITCH: I didn't know your name, but yes.

MIKE: And you thought that was okay?

MITCH: You kill people for him.

MIKE: Lots of people kill for Dominic. But I'm a specialist. I'm so good at making people die, I'm practically an artist. There has to be a good reason for Dominic to call me in.

MITCH: I told him someone was sleeping with my wife and I wanted them dead and it had to be discreet.

MIKE: So he doesn't know about your plan?

MITCH: He wouldn't have set up this meeting if he did.

MIKE: How long have you known about Susan and I?

MITCH: Three months.

MIKE: That's a long time to lie in waiting. How'd you find out?

MITCH: I saw a text message.

MIKE: What did it say?

MITCH: I'd rather not say.

MIKE: I'm not asking.

MITCH: "I want your cock inside me right now."

(MIKE *pistol whips* MITCH *in the head.* MITCH *falls to the ground.*)

MIKE: Susan would never say the word "cock".

MITCH: Are you enjoying this?

MIKE: Enjoying what?

MITCH: Torturing me.

MIKE: Let me assure you Mitch. This is not torture. I don't want to inflict pain on you. But we need to get to a place where you and I are being completely honest.

MITCH: What more do you need to know?

MIKE: Tell me about the money.

MITCH: What money?

MIKE: The money that used to be in your bank account but is now gone.

MITCH: How do you—

MIKE: Did I not just say I've been in your office?

MITCH: That envelope is the last of it.

MIKE: You don't have any investments? Stocks? Life insurance?

MITCH: Gone.

MIKE: Where did it all go?

MITCH: Does it really matter?

(MIKE *pulls the trigger. It goes click.*)

MITCH: I had debts!!

MIKE: To Dominic?

MITCH: Yes!!

MIKE: How much do you still owe him?

MITCH: *(Beat)* More than I have.

MIKE: Does Susan know any of this?

MITCH: No.

MIKE: Thank you. That's all I needed to know.

MITCH: I'm not a bad guy, you know. At one time I considered myself a decent person.

MIKE: Do you remember when we first met?

MITCH: I didn't know we had.

MIKE: It was a year ago. A holiday party thrown by our mutual friend. You were sitting at the bar drinking scotch, watching the Rangers game. I sat and had one with you. We began talking as guys at a bar often do. Exchanging pleasantries, providing commentary on the dismal Rangers.

MITCH: I don't recall that at all.

MIKE: You were very drunk. *(Beat)* Then she came over.

MITCH: Susan?

MIKE: She was tired and wanted to leave. She was wearing this red dress. You introduced us. *(Beat)* I remember looking into her eyes, and it was like time stopped. My cheeks went flush. My palms began to sweat. I felt like a little schoolboy. Susan saw that. And she smiled. For the first time I felt real joy. Almost as if I'd lived my entire life just to get to that moment. The moment where I met the person who made me see the world in a new light.

MITCH: Look, if you're going to kill me can you please just do it?

MIKE: *(Beat)* I've got a lot of money. More than enough to erase your debts.

MITCH: Why would you help me?

MIKE: Helping you insinuates that I'd be giving you something for nothing. Which is not what I'm proposing.

MITCH: Then what are you proposing?

MIKE: A transaction.

MITCH: What would this transaction entail?

MIKE: I make your problems go away. You leave and never come back.

MITCH: Like I pack a bag and get on a plane?

MIKE: Like you fake your death.

MITCH: Nobody fakes their own death and gets away with it.

MIKE: I didn't realize you were an expert on the subject.

MITCH: I'm just saying in this day and age with paper trails and digital footprints.

MIKE: Which is why I would help you. I know people. They'll set you up with a new identity, passports, birth certificates, A home, a 401K, they'll even give you a dog. No cats though.

MITCH: I could never leave.

MIKE: Why not?

MITCH: Because I have a life here.

MIKE: You've got a target on your back, no money, a wife who hates you—

MITCH: Susan loves me.

MIKE: No Mitch. Susan loves me. Now take my offer or I'm killing you.

MITCH: I have to think.

MIKE: Yes or no?!

MITCH: Yes!

(Beat)

MIKE: I need your wallet, car keys, wrist watch and phone.

MITCH: This watch is a family heirloom.

(Pause. MITCH *takes off the watch and puts it on the table along with his keys, wallet and phone.)*

MITCH: What happens now?

*(*MIKE *jabs a needle into* MITCH's *thigh.)*

MIKE: You'll be passing out shortly.

MITCH: No. I don't want to—

*(*MITCH *tries to get up but falls to the ground. After a moment he begins to breathe heavy.)*

MIKE: Do you feel it?

MITCH: Yes.

MIKE: How does it feel?

MITCH: It feels, comfortable. *(Beat)* Like a waaarm current.

MIKE: That's very poetic.

MITCH: I…always liked…poetry. *(He passes out.)*

Scene 2

(A day later. A bare room in a house upstate. A table with a bottle of whiskey, two glasses and a small beat up stereo. A chair next to the table. MITCH *is laying on the ground, sleeping. He has a bandage on his head.)*

(After a moment MITCH *wakes up in a dazed fashion and tries to get a grip on his surroundings.)*

(The door opens and MIKE *enters with a plastic shopping bag and a small briefcase. The two men look at one another.)*

MIKE: I was wondering when you were going to wake up.

MITCH: How long have I been out?

(MIKE *puts the plastic bag on the chair and sets the briefcase on the floor next it.*)

MIKE: About fifteen hours.

MITCH: That shot you gave me must've been strong.

MIKE: It's a drug used to sedate a large animals.

MITCH: Where are we?

MIKE: A place off the Taconic. Lots of escape routes, clean, empty. *(Beat)* I brought food.

MITCH: What do you have?

MIKE: Some peanut butter, granola bars. A strawberry banana smoothie.

MITCH: I'll take a granola bar.

(MIKE *passes* MITCH *a granola bar.*)

MIKE: How does your head feel?

MITCH: It hurts like hell.

MIKE: Lets take a look. Do you like music?

MITCH: Sure.

(MIKE *goes to the stereo and turns it on. Classical music lightly begins to play. Bach's "The Brandenburg Concerto".*)

MIKE: I find most situations in life fairly stressful so I gravitate toward things that relax me.

(MIKE *goes to* MITCH *and starts to examine the wound and put on a new bandage.*)

MITCH: Is this Bach?

MIKE: The Brandenburg Concerto. *(Beat)* He's one of my favorites. Came from a family full of great composers but he was never considered one himself. It wasn't until fifty years after his death that his music caught on. *(Beat)* When I listen to it I hear beauty, complexity, but I also hear such sorrow. The pain of a man who knows his life's work won't be appreciated until long after he's gone.

MITCH: My father used to listen to music like this when he worked.

MIKE: What did he do?

MITCH: He was a writer.

MIKE: Novels?

MITCH: Textbooks. *(Beat)* I don't think he was ever happy.

MIKE: Define happy. *(He finishes with the new bandage.)*

MITCH: Is it done?

Michael goes to the grocery bag and gets a newspaper and hands it to Mitch.

MIKE: The story is on page three.

MITCH: "In a press conference the mayor decreed that March 16th will be known citywide as Cat Appreciation Day."

MIKE: The other story.

MITCH: "Police investigators are still trying to piece together the events on the FDR yesterday morning, when a Lexus sedan swerved off the road and plunged into the east River. Divers located the car, which didn't contain a body. Found inside was a wallet belonging to the owner of the car, New Jersey resident Mitchell Cohen, who is believed to be…"

(MITCH puts down the paper. Pause)

MIKE: You don't exactly seem excited.

MITCH: I just found out I'm dead. How do you want me to react?

MIKE: Actually you're not dead until they call off the search. And how about reacting with a little gratitude? Do you know how hard it is to flip a mid size sedan off the FDR?

MITCH: Excuse me but I didn't ask you to flip my car off the road. *(Beat. Then calmer)* It's just that things are so unresolved.

MIKE: When people die that tends to happen.

MITCH: I don't have a will. No insurance. There's going to be loan sharks.

MIKE: I'm going to handle all of that.

MITCH: What about my funeral?

MIKE: What about it?

MITCH: A funeral is a major undertaking. The flowers alone cost thousands. And the casket? Not to mention a decent cemetery plot.

MIKE: It's a stone with your name on it.

MITCH: You gotta find me good location.

MIKE: Does it really matter?

MITCH: Of course it matters. I mean I don't want to be all crowded in or off in some corner, or even worse stuck next to the road. I want to be in a nice shaded area, maybe even on top of a hill or something.

MIKE: *(Mildly irritated)* I'll get you the nicest plot money can buy, alright?

MITCH: I'm sorry if I'm irritating you but this is a lot to digest. I mean when my casket is lowered into the grave what's gonna even be in there?

MIKE: Probably nothing.

MITCH: My casket is going to be empty??

MIKE: The casket being empty is the point!

MITCH: *(Beat)* What about Susan?

MIKE: What about Susan?

MITCH: Have you talked to her?

MIKE: I need to stay away until the police rule her out as a suspect.

MITCH: They don't think she would actually—

MIKE: When a person dies the police always look at the spouse. Just a formality.

MITCH: She must be devastated.

MIKE: Probably.

MITCH: Devastated and terrified.

MIKE: What she is or isn't is no longer your concern.

MITCH: I can't help how I feel. And I didn't exactly come up with this plan.

MIKE: You're not having second thoughts, are you Mitch?

MITCH: It's just that I didn't say goodbye. *(Beat)* Normally she would wake up before me. Early riser. But yesterday I got up first. Got dressed. Went down to the kitchen. Waited for her. She came down in her robe with this puzzled look on her face. She asked what I was doing up so early. I wanted to say so many things. But all I said was that I had a meeting. She went back up stairs. And I left.

(Beat)

MIKE: I want to tell you something.

MITCH: What?

MIKE: I envy you.

MITCH: I just gave up everything.

MIKE: You're still a young man. You're getting a fresh start. Do you know how many people would kill to be in your shoes?

MITCH: I wanted to make her happy. I wanted it so badly. But I just couldn't. *(Beat)* Does she know what you do?

MIKE: She thinks I'm a dentist.

MITCH: Maybe that's why she started seeing you. I hate the dentist. *(Beat)* Can I ask you something?

MIKE: Shoot.

MITCH: Why Susan?

MIKE: I love her.

MITCH: But what draws you to her?

MIKE: Put your shoes on Mitch.

MITCH: *(Beat)* So. What do we do now?

MIKE: Right. There's a man sitting in a car out front. A friend of mine. He's waiting for me to leave. When I do he'll come to the door and knock three times. Knock. Knock. Knock. Then you pick up your briefcase, you open the door, and you leave.

MITCH: I don't have a briefcase.

MIKE: You do now. *(He motions to the briefcase.)*

MITCH: What's inside?

MIKE: Money.

MITCH: How much?

MIKE: Enough.

(Beat)

MITCH: Where am I going?

MIKE: I don't know. It's better that way.

MITCH: *(Beat)* Do you think I could have my gun back?

MIKE: Why?

MITCH: Protection.

MIKE: From what?

MITCH: …I don't even know.

MIKE: *(A pause)* Well I should—

MITCH: Yes. Okay.

MIKE: Heading back they've got the right lane closed for construction to Newburgh. Total nightmare.

MITCH: I can imagine.

MIKE: *(Beat)* Good luck with everything. I sincerely mean that.

MITCH: You too.

(MIKE and MITCH shake hands.)

MIKE: Mitch? Don't ever come back.

(MIKE stares at MITCH for a moment to drive the point home, then exits.)

(A moment. MITCH looks at the briefcase and considers the fact that it might be empty and that this could actually be a set up. He goes to the briefcase and puts it on the table. He un-clips the locks, pauses a moment, then opens it. It's full of money. He exhales. Suddenly three knocks at the door. It gives him a jolt. He looks at the door a moment, then he closes the briefcase and picks it up. He walks to the door, hesitates a moment, then opens it and exits. Lights fade.)

Scene 3

(A few days later inside the living room of MITCH and SUSAN. It's contemporary and nicely furnished. The room is dim and we see the flicker of a television glowing off the face of her, an attractive mid thirty something women, who is curled up on the couch. There is a knock on the door. SUSAN

goes to the door. MICHAEL *is standing there. He's holding a bottle of wine.)*

SUSAN: He's dead.

MIKE: I know. I saw the news. *(Beat)* Can I? *(Come in.)*

(Beat. SUSAN *nods.)*

*(*MIKE *enters.)*

MIKE: How are you feeling?

SUSAN: Four days ago my husband drove his car into the river. *(She goes back to the couch and plops down.)*

MIKE: Were you sleeping?

SUSAN: I was watching TV.

MIKE: Anything good on?

SUSAN: Manhattan.

MIKE: That's a good one. I prefer Celebrity.

SUSAN: I tried calling you.

MIKE: When?

SUSAN: Yesterday and the day before. You didn't pick up.

MIKE: My phone was off.

SUSAN: Why?

MIKE: It died. I thought I lost the thing. This morning I found it lodged in my car seat. I would've come over sooner, but I figured with everything—

SUSAN: It's for the best that you didn't. This week has been indescribable.

MIKE: I can't imagine.

SUSAN: Monday afternoon there was a knock on the door. This cop is standing there. Sargent Peters. In this robot voice he informs me my husband's car careened into the East River and that they are searching for him but he's presumed dead. No "I'm sorry". No sympathy. He only asked to come inside so he could search through Mitch's things.

MIKE: Why?

SUSAN: To see if he was taking any drugs or was on medication.

MIKE: Was he?

SUSAN: No. They don't think it was an accident. They think…

MIKE: What do you think happened?

SUSAN: I don't know. *(Beat)* Most mornings he'd just leave without saying anything. But that day I came downstairs and he was sitting at the kitchen table, waiting for me. There was this look in his eyes. Like he was about to do something.

(Beat)

MIKE: I know it doesn't seem like it now, but maybe all of this is for the best.

SUSAN: How?

MIKE: Not that this isn't a tragedy. But now you can finally move on with things.

SUSAN: What things?

MIKE: We had plans.

SUSAN: Plans.

MIKE: We talked about you leaving him.

SUSAN: I can't think about that right now.

MIKE: I'm not asking you to.

SUSAN: I mean, yes, I wasn't happy. But I didn't want him to die.

MIKE: Of course you didn't. *(Beat)* I can't imagine what you're going through.

SUSAN: It's just this whole thing is so odd. You can be stuck in the most hopeless situation. Day after day you pray for relief. Then it comes. And you don't feel relief at all.

(Pause)

MIKE: Look. I should go.

SUSAN: No you don't have to.

MIKE: You need some space to digest what's happened—

SUSAN: Please stay. I want you to. *(Beat)* I can't do this on my own.

MIKE: You don't have to.

SUSAN: Now that he's officially dead I'm starting to plan the funeral. There's so many details and decisions that need to be made. It's so expensive. Not that I care how much it cost. I mean insurance should pay for that, right?

MIKE: Right.

SUSAN: Wrong. This morning I called the insurance company. They told me his life insurance policy was cancelled a year ago.

MIKE: Cancelled?

SUSAN: It was a million dollar policy, Mike. And now it's just gone.

MIKE: You had no idea?

SUSAN: None. He insisted on handling all of that stuff. Then I went to the bank to check our savings. According to them all I have left is one thousand dollars and sixty-seven cents.

MIKE: Look. You don't have to worry about any of this.

SUSAN: How can I not worry? I have no money. I have bills, I need to buy food. I need fucking toilet paper. And this goddman funeral is going to cost ten thousand dollars alone.

MIKE: I'll pay for it.

SUSAN: *(Beat)* What?

MIKE: Tell me what you need and I'll handle it.

SUSAN: Okay, I am not asking you to do that.

MIKE: I know you're not.

SUSAN: This is not your problem.

MIKE: I know it's not.

SUSAN: Mike I don't want your charity.

MIKE: This is not charity. Do you remember the night we first met?

SUSAN: Of course. That weird holiday party Mitch dragged me to in the city.

MIKE: Do you remember when we first saw each other?

SUSAN: I was bored and went to Mitch so we could leave and you were sitting with him at the bar.

MIKE: When you came over, you saved me.

SUSAN: How?

MITCH: *(Beat)* I've never told you this, but I was in a bad place in my life and even worse is, I didn't know it. But seeing you, the feeling it gave me, made me realize what I really want. You helped me, Susan, more than anyone ever has. And so helping you now is the least I can do. *(Beat)* If it makes you feel better think of it as a loan.

SUSAN: A loan…

MIKE: And if it helps, I'll charge you a really high interest rate.

SUSAN: Because that's exactly what I need. More debt.

MIKE: Susan please. Let me do this.

(SUSAN *hugs* MIKE.)

SUSAN: I can't tell you how much I need this.

MIKE: I just want you to feel better.

SUSAN: You know what would make me feel better?

MIKE: What?

SUSAN: Getting drunk, watching trashy TV and eating greasy Chinese food.

MIKE: I'm glad I went to the gym earlier.

SUSAN: How are you this perfect?

MIKE: I don't think I'm perfect.

SUSAN: You're damn near close. I mean you're always there when I need you. You're always supportive. And you're so damn positive.

MIKE: You say that like it's a bad thing.

SUSAN: I just don't know if I deserve it.

MIKE: Deserving has got nothing to do with it. You make me happy. Happier than I've even been. No matter what happens I'm not going anywhere. Unless you tell me to. Okay?

SUSAN: I'll open this wine. In the mean time make yourself at home.

(SUSAN *exits with wine.* MIKE *hangs up his coat, then sits down on the couch. He gets comfortable.*)

MIKE: I am home.

(*The lights slowly fade.*)

Scene 4

(It is two years later. We are inside the living room. Which still looks the same. On the couch sits MIKE, *dressed casually reading a book. Perhaps he's wearing a sweater and reading glasses. Fredrick Chopin's "Nocturnes" plays lightly in the background. After a moment we hear the back door open and close.* SUSAN *enters.* MIKE *lowers the book.)*

SUSAN: Hey hun.

*(*MIKE *and* SUSAN *kiss hello.)*

MIKE: You're home later than usual.

SUSAN: I ran by the grocery store, which by the way, I'm now convinced is some type of social experiment. .

MIKE: How so?

SUSAN: The way they make the aisles so narrow, it agitates everyone to the point where they commit passive aggressive acts of violence. Like I was looking at kale and this older women came over and hip checked me out of her way. I look at her and she gives me this little smile and says "oops." I wanted to throw a grape tomato at the back of her head. *(Beat)* How was your day?

MIKE: Busy as always. You?

SUSAN: Just work.

MIKE: And how was it?

SUSAN: Slow.

MIKE: That's nice.

SUSAN: Not really. When it's slow it's kinda like being tortured. Like I can actually feel my skin starting to wrinkle.

MIKE: I thought you liked your job?

SUSAN: I mean I don't hate it. But there are days when I leave that place and I ask myself "what am I doing with my life?" And to be honest, aside from working a desk job, and having health insurance, I don't know that I'm doing anything worthwhile.

MIKE: Maybe you should quit.

SUSAN: If I did what would I do with myself?

MIKE: You could take up a hobby.

SUSAN: Or I could help you.

MIKE: What?

SUSAN: Down at your office. I could be your receptionist.

MIKE: You would hate it.

SUSAN: Come on. I'd answer your calls. Make you your coffee. I could even wear a little nurse's uniform?

MIKE: *(Pivoting.)* For the record receptionists don't wear nurses uniforms. But I'll take it under consideration.

(Beat)

SUSAN: I'm gonna put away the groceries and open some wine. Want a glass?

MIKE: Yep.

(SUSAN begins to exit.)

SUSAN: Oh. Did you notice the back screen door?

MIKE: I fixed it last week.

SUSAN: I know. But this morning I opened it and there it was again. A little hole bored through the bottom.

MIKE: Probably another mouse.

SUSAN: I don't think it's a mouse. It looks like teeth marks.

MIKE: Perhaps it's a rat.

SUSAN: A rat?

MIKE: This time of year they look for warm shelter. *(Beat)* Not that it's that. I'm just saying.

SUSAN: Call the exterminator. Please.

MIKE: I'm on it.

(Beat)

(SUSAN exits. MIKE resumes reading. Then something catches his attention. He puts down the book and tunes into the environment.)

(He gets up. He slowly walks to the door. He opens it. There's nothing there. She enters with two glasses of wine.)

SUSAN: What are you doing?

MIKE: I thought I heard something.

SUSAN: What?

MIKE: I'm not sure.

SUSAN: Maybe it was the rat.

MIKE: Maybe. *(He closes the door and walks back to the couch.)*

(SUSAN gives MIKE his glass.)

SUSAN: It's a merlot.

MIKE: Cheers.

SUSAN: Cheers.

(MIKE and SUSAN clink glasses and drink. A pause. She looks like something is on her mind.)

MIKE: Hey everything okay?

SUSAN: Sure. Why?

MIKE: For a moment you looked sad.

SUSAN: I was just thinking.

MIKE: About what?

SUSAN: Nothing. Sorry.

MIKE: I'm wondering if you've given any more thought to what we've been talking about.

SUSAN: What have we been talking about?

MIKE: About children.

SUSAN: Sure. *(Beat)* I've thought about it.

MIKE: And?

SUSAN: It's not that I don't like the thought. But I'm not sure this is the right time.

MIKE: Of course it is.

SUSAN: How so?

MIKE: We're both at ideal ages where we're mature enough to handle the responsibility yet young enough to endure the sleepless nights.

SUSAN: That's exactly my point. Having a child shouldn't be about enduring anything. It should be about love and patience and endless affection.

MIKE: And it will be. We just have to make that leap.

SUSAN: When we first met, you told me you weren't sure if you wanted kids. But lately it's like all you can talk about is having a family.

MIKE: It's what people in our position do.

SUSAN: We've been married barely a year.

MIKE: Exactly. Married couples spend the first year or so having wild and spontaneous sex, showering each other with passion and romance. And then they settle in and tone things down.

SUSAN: Is that your way of telling me to trade in the lingerie for mom jeans?

MIKE: I'm referring to the grander scheme of things. I'm talking about our future. Us growing further into our roles.

SUSAN: What roles would those be?

MIKE: I'm the patriarch and you're the matriarch. I provide and you nurture.

SUSAN: I'm the one who bakes the apple pies and you're the one who coaches the tee ball games?

MIKE: That's a little cliche, but sure.

SUSAN: I can see it now, Mike. Our child, he or she, stepping up to the plate and knocking one right into the out field. The crowd going wild as they round the bases. And right before they cross home plate we look at one another with pride and hold hands. Cause our dream has come true.

MIKE: I sense that you're holding back.

SUSAN: I can't help it. This is so, silly.

MIKE: Why? I have a stable job. We have a house that's paid for. We even have an empty room upstairs just waiting to be a nursery.

SUSAN: I know we do.

MIKE: I come home every day and it's wonderful. We have a great routine. We pour a glass of wine, talk about our day. We have a lovely dinner. *(Beat)* We've never even had a serious fight.

SUSAN: We had one.

MIKE: When?

SUSAN: When you wanted us to move.

MIKE: I just thought living here as a married couple after what happened wasn't the healthiest thing for either of us.

SUSAN: I wasn't ready to leave.

MIKE: I know you weren't. And now I love it here as much as you do. I finally have space for my stuff. My books, my pictures—

SUSAN: Your mysterious little lock box.

MIKE: What box is that?

SUSAN: The one in our bedroom closet.

MIKE: There's nothing mysterious about that box. I told you that's where I keep tax records.

SUSAN: In a box that's locked?

MIKE: So I don't lose any of my returns. You want to look in the box? I'll go get it.

SUSAN: Mike. Forget the box.

MIKE: This is so silly. We never bicker over petty things. We always compromise with each other. I don't want to brag, but I think we have a near perfect relationship.

SUSAN: I think it's pretty great too.

MIKE: Then what's the problem? That there is no problem?

SUSAN: That's not a problem.

MIKE: Exactly. So when do you want to have kids?

SUSAN: I don't know.

MIKE: Five months?

SUSAN: I don't know.

MIKE: A year?

SUSAN: I don't know.

MIKE: Two years?

SUSAN: I don't know if I want kids!

(Pause)

MIKE: You did before.

(MIKE *finishes his wine, gets up and turns off the music.*)

SUSAN: It's not that I never wanted kids. I just don't know that I want them now.

MIKE: I don't understand. When we first got married you used to sit at breakfast and think up endless lists of names. And now suddenly—

SUSAN: I know I'm acting weird, okay? *(Beat)* It's just been a strange day.

MIKE: Tell me what happened.

SUSAN: I don't know if I should.

MIKE: Susan.

(Beat)

SUSAN: I thought I saw someone.

MIKE: Who?

SUSAN: Mitch.

MIKE: Mitch as in your dead ex-husband?

SUSAN: I was in the park by work eating lunch. I noticed this guy further down the path. He was wearing a hat that covered part of his face. But I really think it was him. *(Beat)* You think I'm a lunatic, don't you?

MIKE: Of course not. I see people who remind me of people I know all the time.

SUSAN: This wasn't that. It was him.

MIKE: But that's impossible. He's been dead for nearly two years.

SUSAN: I know. But what if he isn't?

MIKE: Susan…

SUSAN: I mean they never found his body.

MIKE: What did the police report say?

SUSAN: That he was more than likely thrown from the vehicle and the current carried him away.

MIKE: Exactly.

SUSAN: I see a man who looks exactly like Mitch sitting in the park and you don't find it odd?

MIKE: You know what I find odd? That I'm trying to have a conversation about us starting a family and all you want to do is talk about your dead husband.

SUSAN: You don't have to get upset.

MIKE: I can't help it. The man was a degenerate. He left you with nothing.

SUSAN: With all do respect what happened between me and him is none of you business. *(Beat)* I'm sorry.

MIKE: You don't have to apologize.

SUSAN: I'm biting your head off for no reason.

MIKE: I just want to see you happy.

SUSAN: I am happy. And I'm grateful that you're in my life.

MIKE: You don't have to say that.

SUSAN: You're kind. And honest. And smart. And sweet.

MIKE: Okay…

SUSAN: And loyal. And you have really great teeth.

MIKE: Now you're just telling me what I want to hear.

SUSAN: You really are the greatest thing to happen to me. I want you to know that.

MIKE: I do.

SUSAN: So you're not mad at me?

MIKE: I could never be mad at you. Even when I'm mad at you.

(Beat)

SUSAN: I'll get dinner started.

MIKE: You want company? I can be your sous chef.

SUSAN: I've got it. You keep relaxing.

MIKE: What are we having?

SUSAN: Braised chicken and gazpacho.

MIKE: Sounds delicious.

(SUSAN starts to head to the kitchen.)

SUSAN: Maybe it was just a memory.

MIKE: What was?

SUSAN: When Mitch and I were first married we used to meet in that park for lunch.

MIKE: I guess it's just a memory then.

(SUSAN exits to the kitchen. MIKE sits for a moment. Then he looks to the door. Lights fade.)

Scene 5

(The next day. At the park outside SUSAN's work. MITCH, now with shaggier hair, sits at a bench. He is dressed casually. Perhaps he also has a bit of a sun tan. There is a calmness about him that wasn't present before.)

(After a moment SUSAN enters from behind. She stands frozen and watches him.)

(MITCH senses her presence but he doesn't turn around and face her.)

SUSAN: Is it you?

(MITCH stands and faces her. SUSAN slowly walks over.)

SUSAN: It is you. I can't believe it.

MITCH: What can't you believe?

SUSAN: That you're actually standing here.

MITCH: You're very pale. Like you've seen a ghost. *(Beat)* That was a joke.

SUSAN: Where am I from?

MITCH: What?

SUSAN: I don't know if I fully believe you're you.

MITCH: How could I not be me?

SUSAN: You've been dead two years.

MITCH: You're from Canton. *(Beat)* Ohio.

SUSAN: What street did I grow up on?

MITCH: Franklin.

SUSAN: *(Beat)* What color was my bedroom wallpaper in my college dorm?

MITCH: What?

SUSAN: You heard me.

MITCH: The wallpaper was green. Your sheets were blue. And you had a roommate named Marla who made you pray before bed every night.

SUSAN: Her name was Martha.

MITCH: It's been a while.

SUSAN: What instrument did she play?

MITCH: Really Susan?

SUSAN: Yes really!

MITCH: Marla played the flute. Terribly.

(SUSAN *walks up to* MITCH. *She hesitantly touches his face. Almost a poke. Then she hugs him.*)

MITCH: It's nice to feel your embrace.

(SUSAN *lets go of the hug and slaps* MITCH.)

SUSAN: You're supposed to be dead, Mitch!

MITCH: I know.

SUSAN: The police said you—

MITCH: I know what they said.

SUSAN: This whole time I thought you were dead. And then yesterday.

MITCH: I didn't know if you still worked here or not. I was hoping you didn't. I've always thought you were overqualified for secretarial work.

(Beat)

SUSAN: This is very jarring.

MITCH: I can understand that.

SUSAN: I don't know how to feel. I don't know what to say. I don't know whether to laugh or cry or scream.

MITCH: Well, you might not want to scream, but that's just me.

SUSAN: Where have you been?

MITCH: All over the world. Asia. South Africa. Alaska. I lived in Barcelona for a few months. Beautiful city. (Beat) I know this is wild, and I don't want to overwhelm you, but for what it's worth, it's really nice to see you.

SUSAN: Is it?

MITCH: You look really great.

SUSAN: Oh, a compliment.

MITCH: What are you thinking?

SUSAN: I'm wondering what even happened with your death. You could barely color coordinate your socks, let alone pull off a stunt like that.

MITCH: You could say I got some help.

SUSAN: *(Beat)* So why are you here? I mean doesn't returning home go against the rules of "faking your own death" thing?

MITCH: I don't think there's a rule book when it comes to these things. But I wanted to talk to you.

SUSAN: We have nothing to talk about.

MITCH: Then why'd you come back today?

SUSAN: This is my park. I come here every day.

MITCH: Since you first started working here. Back then we were so broke we could barely afford rent much less food. But still. Every second Friday I'd come down here after getting my paycheck. I'd pick up your favorite cheese and some olives from the that cafe by my office. I'd bring them here and we'd have a nice lunch.

SUSAN: Taking a trip down memory lane…

MITCH: I'm just saying we both loved that.

SUSAN: You left me with no insurance. No stocks. No money. You left me completely helpless.

MITCH: I know I made a ton of mistakes.

SUSAN: Really? What mistakes have you made?

MITCH: Would you like me to list them one by one?

SUSAN: Yes.

MITCH: For starters I didn't communicate my feelings. I wasn't sensitive to the needs of others. I ran from my problems. I neglected you. I was a self absorbed narcissist.

SUSAN: But you're not anymore?

MITCH: No. I still am. But I'm working on it.

SUSAN: You still have redundant grammar. *(Beat)* A narcissist is someone who's self absorbed.

MITCH: Can I ask how you've been?

SUSAN: I got re-married.

MITCH: When?

SUSAN: A year ago.

MITCH: Any kids?

SUSAN: No.

MITCH: I'm surprised. When we were together that's all you could talk about. *(Beat)* Did you move or are you still living in our house?

SUSAN: I'm still there.

MITCH: How does your husband feel about that?

SUSAN: He loves it.

MITCH: I'm glad to hear it. A man should love where he calls home. But still, a man should make his own home, don't you think?

(SUSAN *slaps* MITCH.)

SUSAN: That's for making me miss you.

MITCH: I thought when you heard I died you wouldn't care.

SUSAN: Well I did.

(Beat)

MITCH: What was my funeral like?

SUSAN: You mean the funeral that I couldn't pay for because you cancelled our insurance?

MITCH: Yes.

SUSAN: It was nice. It was a sunny day. There were lots of people there. More than I thought there'd be.

MITCH: Where was the service?

SUSAN: Saint Christopher's.

MITCH: The church we got married in.

SUSAN: Seemed appropriate. *(Beat)* Even though there wasn't a body we got you a casket anyway.

MITCH: Where's it buried?

SUSAN: In a shaded area on top of a hill.

MITCH: Sounds expensive.

SUSAN: It was.

MITCH: Who paid for it?

SUSAN: Mitch, what's the point of this questioning?

MITCH: Remember what we were like in college? We had all these plans. I wanted to be a record producer. And you wanted to be an actress.

SUSAN: It was a pipe dream.

MITCH: It was an ambition. I remember watching you act. You were so full of life. So full of joy. You were aware of the world and you wanted to see it.

SUSAN: That was a long time ago.

MITCH: The world is still out there Susan. You can still see it. All you have to do is go.

SUSAN: Why'd you fake your death?

MITCH: It's, complicated.

SUSAN: Want to hear something funny? I thought you killed yourself to get away from me.

MITCH: Nothing could be further from the truth.

SUSAN: Where did all our money go?

MITCH: Debts.

SUSAN: To who?

MITCH: To some very bad people. The debts I had to them I couldn't pay. I got in over my head. *(Beat)* I wanted to tell you.

SUSAN: Then why didn't you?

MITCH: I thought you wouldn't understand.

SUSAN: So you thought it better to drive your car off the freeway.

MITCH: I wasn't thinking.

SUSAN: Clearly not. *(Beat)* I knew you were into something. I just didn't know what. You'd come home and it's like you weren't even there. I'd ask what was wrong but you'd just get angry. So I stopped asking.

MITCH: I want you to know I'd give anything to take it back.

SUSAN: It no longer matters. Because I'm re-married. Happily.

(Beat)

MITCH: Tell me about your husband.

SUSAN: What do you want to know?

MITCH: What's his name?

SUSAN: Mike.

MITCH: *(Beat)* Tell me. What does Mike do for a living?

SUSAN: He's a dentist.

MITCH: How long has Mike been a dentist?

SUSAN: What's the point of this, Mitch? Why are you asking me this?? Why the hell are you here??

MITCH: I feel an obligation to tell you things that you need to know.

SUSAN: What things?

(Beat)

MITCH: Susan, I don't know the best way to put this. So I'm just going to say it. Your husband is not who you think he is.

SUSAN: Is that so?

MITCH: It is. And I don't know what he's told you but I'm willing to bet almost all of it is complete lies.

SUSAN: Like what?

MITCH: Well I know for a fact that he isn't a dentist.

SUSAN: My husband, who has always been there for me, and has never given me a reason to doubt him, is not a dentist?

MITCH: That's what I'm saying.

(Beat)

SUSAN: Okay, Mitch. I'll bite. What is he?

MITCH: I don't know what he is now, but I know what he used to be.

SUSAN: And what's that?

MITCH: A contract killer.

SUSAN: …In what sense was he a contract killer?

MITCH: In the sense that he used to kill people professionally.

SUSAN: Mitch…

MITCH: The guy was a specialist, Susan. Like an artist and killing people was his canvas.

SUSAN: It's not that I don't find this entertaining. Because really I do, but for your own sake, go talk to someone. Preferably someone with a PhD in front of their name.

MITCH: I can understand your doubt. But is what I'm telling you so hard to believe? We were married almost fifteen years and you had no clue what I was into. Everyone has secrets, Susan. It's just some of us are better at hiding them than others.

SUSAN: How would you even know what my husband does or doesn't do? You've never met him.

MITCH: You and him were having an affair.

SUSAN: You knew about that?

MITCH: Of course I knew! You weren't even trying to cover it up.

SUSAN: Why would try to cover it up when you clearly didn't care?

MITCH: You were my wife. Of course I cared!

SUSAN: That doesn't explain how you'd know my husband is a professional killer.

MITCH: I know he's a killer because I hired him to kill you.

SUSAN: What??

MITCH: I wasn't actually going to have you killed. It was just my cover story for getting him to meet me. So I could kill him. The thought of him being with you was destroying me. I needed to take a stand.

SUSAN: By killing him?

MITCH: In retrospect it was an impulsive choice.

SUSAN: Look. I'm happy, you're crazy and my husband is not a professional killer. End of discussion. Good bye.

MITCH: Do you know where he's from?

SUSAN: Of course I do.

MITCH: Have you ever visited? Have you ever met his friends? Have you met his family?

SUSAN: His family is deceased.

MITCH: The entire family?

SUSAN: Yes.

MITCH: I don't know about you, but that strikes me as a little convenient.

SUSAN: People die, Mitch.

MITCH: They certainly do. Especially around your husband.

SUSAN: If he were a professional killer, and you were going to kill him, why didn't he kill you?

MITCH: I think he felt bad for me. He knew my plan and was waiting for me. He had me admit everything I'd done. The laundering, spending all our money, ruining everything you and I had worked for. When I was finished, he told me I had a choice. I could either die right there or he'd help me fake my own death.

SUSAN: What?

MITCH: I didn't want to do it. I wanted to return to you. Make things right. Try to become the man I wanted to be. But he wanted you for himself.

SUSAN: Stop it.

MITCH: After I agreed to disappear, he injected me with this knock out drug. And while I slept in some house upstate he flipped my car off the FDR. With my wallet, phone and wristwatch inside.

SUSAN: Stop it, Mitch.

MITCH: When I woke up he showed me the article. I saw the picture of the crane lifting my car out of the river. I couldn't believe how there was already algae on the door panels.

SUSAN: Why are you doing this?

MITCH: Because I still love you. And despite everything that's happened, I think I can still make you happy.

SUSAN: Mitch.

MITCH: We were happy once, weren't we? Before all of this. We were so happy. And that's all that mattered. I want to get back to that place. All we'd have to do is leave.

SUSAN: Get away from me.

(SUSAN tries to walk away. MITCH grabs her arm.)

MITCH: I have money. We can go anywhere.

SUSAN: Let go of my arm before I scream.

(MITCH lets go of SUSAN's arm. She begins to walk away.)

MITCH: His favorite composer is Bach. *(Beat)* He likes all classical music but Bach resonates with him the most. How would I know that if I didn't know him?

(SUSAN exits. After a moment MITCH sits back down.)

(MIKE enters from behind. He looks at MITCH with a calm seriousness. After a moment MIKE exits.)

(MITCH turns and looks to where MIKE was. He turns back. Lights fade.)

Scene 6

(That afternoon. At the house. SUSAN enters through the front door. She looks troubled.)

SUSAN: Mike? *(To kitchen)* Mike? *(After no response she exits to the bedroom. She returns holding a medium-sized metal lock box. She tries to open it, but it's locked [obviously]. She puts the box on the table and exits to the kitchen. She returns with a knife and goes to pry the box open.)*

(After several attempts SUSAN manages to pry the box open and the top pops up. She slowly opens the box and looks inside. Lights fade.)

Scene 7

(Later that evening. SUSAN is sitting on the couch like she's waiting. The lock box is gone. After a moment the front door opens and MIKE enters. He looks at her a moment. She does not turn to look at him. There is a tension in the air. Then—)

MIKE: *(Trying to be upbeat.)* Hi honey.

SUSAN: *(Looks at him.)* You're home late.

MIKE: I went by the grocery store. I thought I'd make us dinner.

SUSAN: What are we having?

MIKE: Roasted corn paired with peppered pork medallions.

(MIKE walks to SUSAN. He moves in to kiss her. She lets him.)

MIKE: *(Beat)* It's awfully quiet in here.

SUSAN: You don't like the quiet?

MIKE: I just prefer music. Why don't you put some on?

(MIKE exits with groceries. SUSAN goes to the stereo and puts on Bach. He enters with two glasses of wine and a gift bag. He stops and listens to the music.)

MIKE: You put on Bach.

SUSAN: That okay?

MIKE: Sure.

SUSAN: So. Tell me about your day.

MIKE: My day was fine.

SUSAN: Lots of patients?

MIKE: Yes. Kinda. Sorta. Not really.

SUSAN: What are your patients typically like?

MIKE: They vary.

SUSAN: What do most people come to you for?

MIKE: Dental procedures.

SUSAN: Like what?

MIKE: Why are you suddenly so curious about my work?

SUSAN: Because it occurred to me that I really don't know anything about what you do.

MIKE: We can discuss it later. *(Beat)* Here. I got you something.

(MIKE hands SUSAN the gift bag. She pulls out a sizable book.)

SUSAN: The complete works of William Shakespeare. Why would you get me this?

MIKE: I remember you telling me once that you were an actor in college. I thought that maybe you could take it up again.

SUSAN: I thought you wanted to have a child.

MIKE: We can put that on hold. *(Beat)* Life is short. I want you to follow your dreams. *(Beat)* I think I'll go get that dinner started. Oh, you'll be happy to know I found out what was chewing the back screen.

SUSAN: What was it?

MIKE: A stray kitten.

SUSAN: I thought you said it was a rat.

MIKE: I thought it was. But this morning I forgot my wallet, and when I came home, there he was, chewing on the screen with his cute little teeth. When he realized I was standing there he looked up at me with his big round eyes and gave a little meow.

SUSAN: What'd you do with him?

MIKE: I took him over to the vet. Right after I fed the little guy a big bowl of warm milk. Be back shortly.

(MIKE *exits to the kitchen.* SUSAN *reaches in her pocket and pulls out* MITCH's *watch.*)

Mike *(Off)* Say honey?

(Beat)

SUSAN: …Yeah?

MIKE: *(Off)* On the way home it occurred to me that we should go to Ohio.

SUSAN: Why?

MIKE: *(Off)* To visit your parents. The only time I met them was when they came in for our wedding. It'd be nice to get to know them more. Do some quality bonding.

SUSAN: You've never expressed an interest in visiting my family before.

MIKE: *(Off)* I know.

(SUSAN *puts the watch back in her pocket.*)

SUSAN: So why now?

(After a moment MIKE *enters.*)

MIKE: Way I see it we could use a break from our routine. Plus I've never been to Ohio.

SUSAN: I don't think it's a good idea.

MIKE: Hey, I'd say we could visit my parents, but as you know they're dead.

SUSAN: Because they died in a bus accident.

MIKE: That's right.

SUSAN: *(Beat)* I'm confused.

MIKE: About?

SUSAN: I thought you said your parents died in a car accident.

MIKE: They did.

SUSAN: But I just said bus accident.

MIKE: It was a car accident involving a bus.

SUSAN: Mike I want to see your office.

MIKE: Why?

SUSAN: Because I never have and I want to.

MIKE: Okay fine. First thing Monday I'll take you—

SUSAN: I meant now. Right this minute. You can't do that can you? Because it doesn't exist.

(Beat)

MIKE: Susan I want you to know I get it.

SUSAN: Get what?

MIKE: Yesterday in the park, I think you did see Mitch. I also think you went back to the park today and saw him again. Didn't you?

SUSAN: Were you following me?

MIKE: Yes.

SUSAN: Why?

MIKE: Because yesterday you seemed freaked out about thinking you saw your ex so I just wanted to make sure things were alright.

SUSAN: So you followed me.

MIKE: Turns out it was a good idea because the guy showed up again today. *(Beat)* Look, I'm fairly certain your ex husband is a lunatic. I mean he fakes his death two years ago and now he's sitting in the park next to where you work? Does that strike you as the behavior of a rational individual? *(Beat)* He told you stories, didn't he? Stories about how I'm some crazy killer. Stories about how I helped him fake his death.

SUSAN: How do you know he said that?

MIKE: Do I look like a crazy killer?

SUSAN: Look me in the eyes and swear it's not true.

MIKE: Susan. I swear it's not—

Susan reveals a small revolver.

MIKE: Where'd you find that?

SUSAN: Your lock box. I pried it open.

MIKE: That was rude.

SUSAN: Why do you have a gun, Mike?

MIKE: It's for personal protection. I've even got the permit and—

(SUSAN *reveals* MITCH's *watch.*)

MIKE: —everything…

SUSAN: I also found Mitch's watch.

MIKE: That's gonna be a little harder to explain.

SUSAN: Why would you keep this here?

MIKE: What do you mean?

SUSAN: Why would you keep a box containing my former husband's watch in our closet?! I mean what? Is that your way of living on the edge?

MIKE: Please give me the gun.

(SUSAN *levels the gun.*)

SUSAN: I'm going to ask you some questions. And if I think you're lying I'm going to shoot you.

MIKE: Honey do you even know how that thing works?

(SUSAN *pulls back the hammer.*)

SUSAN: Are you a dentist?

MIKE: Technically no. But I am familiar with some procedures.

SUSAN: If you're not a dentist then what do you do during the day?

MIKE: Lots of things. I go to diners. I read all sorts of books. Lately I've been thinking about taking improv classes.

SUSAN: Are you trying to make a joke??

MIKE: I'm just answering your question.

SUSAN: Did you help Mitch fake his death?

MIKE: …Yes.

SUSAN: You drove his car off the road?

MIKE: Not me personally.

SUSAN: But you helped him disappear.

MIKE: Yes.

SUSAN: Jesus.

MIKE: Susan I did it for you.

SUSAN: For me?

MIKE: For us.

SUSAN: So then what he said is true? You are a professional killer?

MIKE: Alright look—

SUSAN: ANSWER ME!!

MIKE: I used to be. Okay?

SUSAN: So what are you now? Just a guy who used to kill people? Is Mike even your real name?

MIKE: Of course it is. (Beat) It's Daniel.

(SUSAN gets up.)

SUSAN: When I met you I thought you were the answer.

MIKE: I am the answer.

SUSAN: You are NOT the answer.

MIKE: You said that I was the greatest thing to ever happen to you!

SUSAN: You just told me that you're a murder!

MIKE: They were all scum bag lowlife degenerates!

SUSAN: *(Beat)* Why'd you let him live?

MIKE: Mitch?

SUSAN: Why didn't you just kill him too?

MIKE: Regardless of my past, I saved you Susan. Mitch, what did he do? He left you with nothing. He pissed away everything and did he tell you? No. He just faked his own death and let me clean up the mess. But let's forget all that. Because I'm the monster. I'm the bad guy.

SUSAN: He said you didn't give him a choice.

MIKE: The man didn't deserve you. Whereas right now you have before you a man who is willing to break himself ten times over in order to give you the world. Just tell me what I have to do and I'll do it.

SUSAN: There's nothing you can do.

MIKE: Then why'd you stay?

SUSAN: When Mitch and I got married my father threw us a huge wedding. I didn't want it, but he wouldn't hear of anything other than giving me the fairy-tale. Mitch and I danced our first dance in front of all those people, and we were looking into each other's eyes, and in that moment I saw our whole future as this place where nothing could ever go wrong. It was an unattainable dream, and that night I fell in love with it. Then when it went wrong, I didn't know how to cope with it, so I pretended everything was fine and I became trapped in my own illusion. And when things got so bad that I thought I was going to shatter, I met you, a man who was kind and strong. You made me feel good again except that I could tell there was something you were hiding. But I ignored it because I still wanted to pretend. I can't pretend any longer. I need to face things, Mike or Dan or whatever your name is. And that is why I stayed.

MIKE: I'm not going to lie- before meeting you I was a bad person. Some would say I was void of conscious. I don't think I was. I just think that I was someone who didn't see another way. But then I met you and suddenly there were possibilities beyond my narrow existence. The moment I laid eyes on you I chose a new path. In you I saw purity.

SUSAN: Purity?

MIKE: Your heart is true. And that's why I love you. I want something good.

SUSAN: I want that too. So I'm going somewhere far away to do something meaningful before it's too late. And if you try to follow me I will kill you.

MIKE: Susan, please.

(MIKE *tries to get up.*)

(SUSAN *shoots* MIKE, *hitting him in the arm. He leans back, clutching his arm.*)

SUSAN: *(Beat)* After opening the box I went to the bank and emptied our account. I just wanted to be honest about that.

MIKE: I guess I just trusted you and figured you were happy.

SUSAN: What?

MIKE: That's why I kept the box in the house.

(SUSAN *exits. Lights fade.*)

Scene 8

(Later that night. The living room is empty. There's a bottle of scotch on the table with two glasses. After a moment MITCH *enters through the open door. He takes in the space, sees his watch and goes too it.* MIKE *enters from the kitchen. He has a bandage wrapped around his arm.)*

MIKE: It was too nice to put in the car.

MITCH: Where's Susan?

MIKE: Gone.

MITCH: What happened?

MIKE: I got shot.

MITCH: Susan shot you?

MIKE: It surprised me too. *(Beat)* The prodigal son returns. Are you armed?

MITCH: Yes.

MIKE: The serial number scratched off?

MITCH: No. I forgot to.

MIKE: It's alright. Just don't throw it in a dumpster after you kill me. *(Beat)* That was a joke.

MITCH: Do you have a gun?

MIKE: Maybe. *(Beat)* You're free to make yourself at home.

MITCH: For the moment I'm fine.

MIKE: What's it like to be back?

MITCH: Strange. Especially this house. It looks the same as the day I left it.

MIKE: I wanted to change it up. Modernize the fixtures. Update those drab curtains upstairs, but Susan wouldn't let me.

MITCH: The woman has very particular tastes.

MIKE: I'm curious. Was that you with the back screen door? You don't have to tell me.

MITCH: I don't know what you're talking about.

(Beat)

MIKE: You look well. I think traveling has done you a world of good.

MITCH: For what it's worth, you don't look so bad yourself. What's with the scotch and two glasses?

MIKE: *(Beat)* That's for us.

MITCH: For us?

MIKE: I've been expecting you. Care for one?

MITCH: A Scotch would be nice.

(MIKE *goes to the scotch and pours two glasses.*)

MIKE: Can I ask you something?

MITCH: Sure.

MIKE: You came back here to win Susan back, yes?

MITCH: Something like that.

MIKE: Did you really think you had a chance? That after all of this, she'd take you back?

MITCH: I thought it was a long shot. But the risk was worth the reward. *(Beat)* You think you and her would've worked out?

MIKE: She didn't want kids. At least with me. And that was going to be a problem.

(MIKE *brings two glasses of scotch and hands one to* MITCH. MITCH *takes it, tentatively.*)

MIKE: To new beginnings.

(MIKE *and* MITCH *clink glasses and take a swig.*)

MITCH: What are you going to do?

MIKE: I suppose I'll do what I always do. Pick up the pieces. Move. Start again. I've lived all over the world. Really no place I haven't been.

MITCH: For what it's worth. I'm sorry.

MIKE: No you're not.

MITCH: No. I guess I'm not.

MIKE: What are you going to do?

MITCH: I don't know. I didn't think that far ahead.

MIKE: Mitch. Always have a plan. Thought you'd of learned that by now.

MITCH: Where are you thinking of moving?

MIKE: I'd like to head somewhere abroad. Exotic. Maybe Caracas.

MITCH: Caracas?

MIKE: Venezuela. The city is only nine miles from the Caribbean Sea but you wouldn't know it. The whole place sits in a valley surrounded by mountains. Very unique. *(Beat)* Truce?

(MIKE extends his hand. MIKE and MITCH shake hands. MIKE jerks MITCH towards him and swings around to MITCH's back, while also twisting MITCH's arm. MITCH drops his drink on the floor.)

MITCH: YHAAAAAW!

MIKE: Never let your guard down. Should've learned that too.

MITCH: Don't break my arm.

MIKE: Then give me the gun.

MITCH: It's in my right pocket!

(MIKE takes the gun. He looks at it.)

MIKE: Seriously. Did you get this from the same fucking guy?

MITCH: I didn't know where else to go.

MIKE: Go to the couch and sit.

(MITCH *goes to the couch.*)

MIKE: Stay there.

(MIKE *picks up* MITCH'*s glass and refills it with scotch. He walks to* MITCH *and hands it to him.* MITCH *takes a sip.*)

MITCH: Are you going to kill me?

MIKE: No. And not because I don't want to. Because I really do.

MITCH: Then why?

MIKE: I'm not that guy any more. And you know what's funny? I wasn't sure of that until just now.

(*A buzzer goes off in the kitchen.*)

MITCH: What was that?

MIKE: Dinner. (*Beat*) You hungry?

MITCH: I could eat.

MIKE: Set the table. Plates are still where they were.

(MIKE *exits.* MITCH *goes to the table and sets three plates.* MIKE *enters with a tray of pork. He looks at the third plate.*)

MITCH: In case she comes back.

MIKE: If she comes back, Mitch, it's not gonna be for dinner. If she walks through that door, we're both real dead.

(MIKE *serves* MITCH *then himself.*)

MITCH: How about music?

MIKE: Any requests?

MITCH: How about Vivaldi?

(MIKE *goes to the stereo. He puts on Vivaldi's "Winter".*)

MIKE: Very talented man, Vivaldi was. A composer and a priest. He had such passion. Passion for life. Passion for music. Passion for God.

MITCH: He had red hair, didn't he?

MIKE: Red like fire. Rare for an Italian.

MITCH: When Susan left, did she say where she was going?

MIKE: No. Just that she wanted to do something good before it was too late. Admirable.

MITCH: Do you think it's too late for us?

MIKE: *(Beat)* What do you think?

MITCH: I think it depends on us.

(MIKE *returns to the table. Before sitting he puts the gun in a spot within both his and* MITCH's *reach. They look at one another.*)

MIKE: If we change our minds.

(*After a moment* MITCH *looks away and returns to his food.* MIKE *watches* MITCH, *and then begins to eat. Music lightly plays.*)

(*Lights slowly fade.*)

END OF PLAY

www.ingramcontent.com/pod-product-compliance
Lightning Source LLC
Chambersburg PA
CBHW070027110426
42741CB00034B/2676